KWANSABAS AND OTHER POEMS

KWANSABAS
AND OTHER POEMS

STEVEN C. THEDFORD

New World Press, Inc
NEXT LEVEL PUBLISHING

Atlanta

2020

This book is dedicated to all the women who have been trailblazers in

the last year that inspired so many Kwansabas

FOREWORD

The Kwansaba is an African American verse form of praise created in 1995 by Eugene B. Redmond, East St. Louis Poet Laureate and professor of English at Southern Illinois-East St. Louis. The poems honor Kwanzaa, a celebration of family and African American culture, and praise writers such as Richard Wright and Sonia Sanchez. The poetic style of the Kwansaba utilizes the number seven, the numeric foundation of Kwanzaa. Thus, a Kwansaba is a heptastich, a poem of seven lines, with seven words in each line, and written with no word exceeding seven letters.

Darline Roy talks about the strict rules of a Kwansaba. The idea was first used by Eugene B. Redmond and refined in the summer workshop of 2015. But there are exceptions to the rule of seven. He agrees that imposing some restriction makes you think about what you are writing. Another example of a kind of poem that has rules is a haiku, a very short form of Japanese poetry in which the first sentence has five syllables, the second line has seven syllables, and the last line has five syllables.

In addition, the Kwansaba poetic form embraces its roots from the South African tradition of the praise poem, called the *izibongo* in Zulu. A praise poem offers veneration to a person, which was popular in the Middle Ages and continues to be embraced in African cultures today. However, the African praise poem is not restricted to this part of the continent and is not uniquely an African motif; it was used during the Renaissance in Europe. Moreover, the praise poem itself is the manifestation of the oral tradition of atavistic songs of the African ancestors.

The "Other Poems" featured in the later part of the book are digressive; they may follow the rules of the Kwansaba but sometimes do not offer praise. The subjects of the poems range from relationships to community.

Kwansabas and Other Poems represents my interpretation of the art form, and hopefully, I have contributed to this particular type of poem, expanding its purview.

Steven C. Thedford

Atlanta, GA, November 2020

TABLE OF CONTENTS

Asya Danielle Branch: Miss Mississippi

Cheslie Kryst: Miss USA

Kaliegh Garris: Miss Teen USA

BLACK GIRL
MAGIC

Nia Franklin: Miss America

Toni-Ann Singh: Miss World

Zozibini Tunzi: Miss Universe

Diahann Carroll

1

Asya Danielle Branch: Miss Mississippi

Embrace your past, you have no say,

even if your parents are locked away

and your home was quickly deemed gray.

Be strong, faithful, humble, and don't delay.

Face your fears and learn to pray.

I help kids so they won't stray.

The new future will be sunny today.

Cheslie Kryst: Miss USA

"The Big Chop"

I ran; I did the big chop.

I wore curls as I talked shop.

I wore a weave, the big plop.

Start with a bun, a dry mop.

I didn't, I let my hair drop.

My career took off, not a stop.

Now, I am the one on top.

Kaliegh Garris: Miss Teen USA

"We are people" 1st.

We are people 1st: young and old.

We are people 1st: black and white.

We are people 1st: short and tall.

We are people 1st: male and female.

We are people 1st: rich and poor.

We are people 1st: deaf and blind.

We are people 1st: nice and kind.

Nia Franklin: Miss America

"My Voice"

During my reign, my voice will ring.

Support the kids who love to sing.

During my reign my voice will ping.

Support the gifted kids who love acting.

During my reign my voice will ding.

Support the kids who love drawing.

During my reign my voice will ting.

Toni-Ann Singh: Miss World

Play the hand life has dealt you.

You don't have cards; become the dealer.

If you aren't that, become the house.

That is what the house does daily.

It's time to change the game anyway.

People admire your unique ability to win.

Give your best and you already won.

Zozibini Tunzi: Miss Universe

"Pretty Brown Girl"

My kind of skin makes me grin.

My kind of curly hair has flair.

My kind of skin does not bend.

My kind of hair won't ever tear.

My kind of skin is my kin.

My kind of hair I always wear.

My kind of skin I won't lend.

Diahann Carroll

Julia, the first African American on TV.

Billy Dee was her husband on *Dynasty*.

Diahann sang the song, "A Sleepin' Bee,"

Won a Tony award with Richard Kiley,

And had a role on *Grey's Anatomy*.

She acted in *Carmen Jones* with Dorothy.

Diahann was an elegant lady—black beauty.

In Memory
Of

Aniah Blanchard

"Shades of Blue"

On your day azul filled the sky,

Blue, your rescue dog, did not cry.

You choose to fight on, not die.

"Baby girl," you were better than pie,

Your nice smile caught your beau's eye,

Life is not fair, but a lie,

We do not want to, but goodbye.

Anthony Hill

"They keep getting away with murder"

It happened again, not guilty of murder.

Cop killed you while you were naked.

He filled your body full of lead

because medicine got you out of bed

He feared for his life, he said.

He could have used his taser instead.

America honors you today, shoots you dead.

Black Lives Matter

Michael Brown, Eric Garner, Ezell Ford, Dante

Parker, Walter Scott, Akai Gurley, Tamir Rice,

Stephon Clark, Eric Harris, Freddie Gray, Sam

Dubose, Jamar Clark, Jeremy McDole, Arther McAfee,

Ronnell Foster, Danny Thomas, Juan Markee, Cynthia

Fields, John Watson, Ariane McCree, Miles Hall

Ahmaud Arbery, Breonna Taylor, George Floyd . . .

Alexandria Ocasio-Cortez – AOC

Ayanna Pressley

THE SQUAD

Ilhan Omar

Rashida Tlaib

A Tale from the Bronx – AOC

The tale begins in a Bronx bar,

Your true words will take you far.

Your patrons taught you how to spar.

Trump hates you because he is subpar.

Keep dancing always to your college guitar.

Thank you for taking on the Czar.

Today, AOC is a rising shining star.

Ayanna Pressley

Your mother's work ethic gave you zeal.

Life toils gave Ayanna nerves of steel.

Too many of us have no meal.

I fight for the people to heal.

I'm in office to satisfy the appeal.

I am known for the green deal.

That is why my color is teal.

Ilhan Omar

Came to America to find the light.

But a racist bully started a fight.

He tried to turn day into night.

However, freedom has given me perfect sight.

Allah has blessed my spirit with might.

The path IIhan has taken helps unite.

Omar, continue to do what is right.

Rashida Tlaib

Voice of people who have no voice.

Knight for persons who had no king.

Protector of the children with no safety.

Voters for citizens who have no vote.

Sponsor of truth nobody wants to hear.

Seeks justice that needs to be sought.

Talib, may peace be upon to you.

Greta Thunberg

Truth is a song to be sung.

The party of hate is your tongue.

Change is coming; a change has begun.

Earth will be saved by the young.

Get out of the way money, Samsung.

Your swan song has played today, rung.

Shame on you, enemy of the sun.

Old-School Nancy

I am Catholic, taught not to hate.

You didn't show up for our date.

I waited, even though you were late.

Why did you hide behind the gate?

I watched until you took the bait.

Why nasty and why did you clate?

I knew you would seal your fate.

Brag Sheet

I need a letter today to compete.

Do you have your new brag sheet?

I have one and I'm a sheik.

I know you are active all week.

I am smart and hard to beat.

I'll write one because you are meek.

I will come by in a week.

Raising Academically Motivated Students

The teacher gave me a zero today.

I got upset; had something to say.

I placed the paper in the tray.

Why you messing with me this way?

My grades must be right; don't play.

We can do this right now, OK.

I strive to be the best, A.

Parents' Care

You are going to this great school

because I am not raising a fool.

Getting good grades is super awesome cool.

Tough classes will prepare a smart tool.

You were chosen from a large pool.

The teacher will tighten your loose spool.

Hard work will make you a jewel.

Black Billionaire

Smith spoke to men at the house.

He came with a bag of cash.

Over the years he became the brass.

Stocks helped him create a large stash.

Paid debt so that it will not last.

The young man danced on the grass.

Tears of joys erupted in the class.

Taking a Knee

Taking a knee, so he can be.

Taking a knee, strong as a tree.

Talking a knee, not a weak plea.

Taking a knee, a slave not free.

Taking a knee, ball on a tee.

Taking a knee, the NFL can't see.

Taking a knee, to find the key.

The New Negro

Rose from slavery like an ancient bennu

The people began to love their hue.

Fought for their rights, what was due.

No time for crying or feeling blue.

Alain Locke coached poets with a clue.

Seek quality was the best new glue.

Real hard work will make us true.

HBCU

A place where we feel we own.

A place where we feel at home.

A place where we enjoy the throne.

A place where we can freely roam.

A place where we laugh and groan.

A place where we can't be cloned.

A place where we're in the zone.

Sandra Lang

I have a story. How to begin?

Born to white parents: that's my kin.

I am colored; I have dark skin.

Africa never knew whether I fit in.

Tried to be Black, just to blend.

Tried to be myself, just to mend.

Being born in Africa was a sin.

OTHER
POEMS

Thank you

Thank you, God, for everything

Thank you for the joy you bring

Thank you, God, for Mom and Dad

Thank you for the fun we had

And thank you for my sister, too

Thank you, God, for being you

you'll never understand

yolanda y. mcmullen

Oct. 4, 1995

you'll never understand why i'm so angry

you'll never understand how a child of five feels being spat on by two white third graders and called a nigger just about every day

you'll never understand how a child of eleven feels when her so-called best friend says to her that the only thing black people know how to do is steal

you'll never understand how it feels to hear someone say that the only thing black people know how to do is have babies

you'll never understand how i feel deep down in my soul and heart every time i see injustices going on in the black community when you tell a nation that's it's okay to rape, beat, and/or kill our black people because their lives are not worth the blood, sweat, and tears that our forefathers built this country with

you'll never understand how it feels to walk into a store and have the security guard follow you because he thinks you're going to steal

you'll never understand how it feels to have people clutch their purses because you on the elevator with them

you'll never understand how it feels to hear "liberty and justice for all" and never see any liberty or justice for African Americans

you'll never understand how it feels to be treated as a second-class citizen until you walk in my skin, then and only then can you tell me you understand

you'll never understand the struggle to be free to hope and pray to live in harmony

my mother cooked and cleaned and took care of you

she wiped your child's noses and breasts and fed them too

my father worked your land with blood, sweat, and tears

and lived his life daily in constant fear

my daughter cared for all your needs

and what did she receive for all her good deeds?

my son wiped and shined your shoes

and later realized in your eyes that's all he'll be able to do

no, you'll never understand the struggle to be free

to live a life of just being black like me

Driving while Black

Driving in Decatur to my job, work.

Cops' light comes on—my car jerks.

The officers had their hands on guns.

I had nowhere to hide or run,

a piece of meat in a bun.

Gave my card, no time for fun.

I was not their favorite, dearest son.

Don't Care

Stared at the kids in class today.

They were playing, cursing, and being risqué.

Males wanted to relax, laugh, and play.

They had no idea they are prey.

Teacher teaches, but only gets a stare.

Student stress causes anger in the air.

As a result, the students don't care.

Better to Cheat than Repeat

In class I'd rather cheat than repeat.

I'll copy the answer from anyone's sheet.

My fake grades allow me to compete.

I hide answers in the calculator case

because I am in a GPA race.

I switch the numbers on the test,

so that people think I'm the best.

El Paso and Dayton

A racist gunman walked into a Walmart.

He shot and killed people with carts.

He showed up in Dayton, Ohio, later:

he was a Mexican and Negro hater,

acting out the text of a beef,

causing carnage, anger, outrage, sorrow, and grief,

doing the direct orders of the chief.

We Did Not Come through Ellis Island

Forced into slavery brought a brutal life,

Forced from their homes by a knife,

Shipped on a cold, dark wet floor,

Chains are what made their hands sore,

No family was waiting on the shore,

These were not choices, but hard labor,

Now we have really endured, God's Favor.

INSPIRATION

November 1956

Although the work is tiring
And the hours are long,
Remember the days of retiring
When you can sing this joyful song.

I have had my share of headaches
And other kinds of misery,
But none of them can outrate
The days I spent in Chemistry.

Although the life I lived was hard,
It greatly aided me
Through the tiresome days and sleepless nights
That led me through Chemistry.

WAIT AND SEE
(January 7, 1956)
(by R. "Ted" Thedford)

I desire little command,
Only a sound destiny
To travel to an unknown land
Ruled by my love and me.

We will rule this land as one
Over all the lovers there
Who have likewise come
To this land with us to share.

Many years have passed and gone,
But still I have that dream
To find a love while alone
And depart into our world unseen.

At times I look above
As if my dream has deceived me,
But then I think of the joy of love
And resolve to wait and see.

Rihanna vs. Chris Brown

The boys sat, as girls went off.

Some girls were on Rihanna's side today.

The other side was for Chris Brown.

Some said real women take a beating;

Rubbish, men should not hit a woman.

Could not believe girls thought this way.

The boys were silent—nothing to say.

References

Brewer, R. (2019, October 18). Kwansaba: Poetic forms. https://www. writersdigest.com/write-better-poetry/kwansaba-poetic-formsBrewer, R. L. (2019, October 18). *Kwansaba: Poetic forms.* https:// www.writersdigest.com/write-better-poetry/kwansaba-poetic-forms

Gorder, J. V. (Tinker). (2017, December 28). *Kwansaba.* http://www. poetrymagnumopus.com/topic/2769-kwansaba/

Johnson, R. N. (2016, April 14). *Kwansaba, a new genre of poetry.* https://www.theodysseyonline.com/kwansaba-genre-poetry

Jones, S. (2010, January 17). In praise of the Kwansaba. *For Southern Boys Who Consider Poetry.* saeedjones.wordpress.com/2009/12/19/ in-praise-of-the-kwansaba/

Kwansaba: Birth of a poetry form. (2008, June 18). http://www.riehlife. com/2008/06/18/kwansaba-birth-of-a-poetry-form/

Kwansaba surprise. (2019, April 10). https://delawaredad. com/2019/04/10/kwansaba-surprise/

Lawrencealot. Kwansaba. (2013, February 25). *Kwansaba.* https:// popularpoetryforms.blogspot.com/2013/02/kwansaba.html.

Redmond, E. B. (2018). Kwansaba: Poets Sonia Sanchez & Jessica Care Moore fly to Planet Ferguson 2015. *Journal of Pan African Studies, 11*(6), 36ff.

Vail, L., & White, L. (1991). *Power and the praise poem: Southern African voices in history*. New York University Press.

9 780975 973059